Everything You Always Wanted to Know About First Grade — But Didn't Know Whom to Ask

by Ellen Booth Church
with Guy N. Fraser

No part of this publication may be reproduced in whole or in part, or stored in a retrieval system, or transmitted in any form or by any means, electronic, mechanical, photocopying, recording, or otherwise, without written permission of the publisher. For information regarding permission, write to Scholastic Inc., 555 Broadway, New York, NY 10012.
Copyright © 1996 by Scholastic Inc.
Illustrations copyright © 1996 by Scholastic Inc.
All rights reserved. Published by Scholastic Inc.
Printed in the U.S.A.
ISBN 0-590-93603-4
1   2   3   4   5   6   7   8   9   10   02   01   00   99   98   97   96

Table of Contents

12. What is the role of writing in first grade, and what is invented spelling all about?

13. What math skills might my child learn in first grade?

14. How will my child explore science in first grade?

15. What is the role of art and music in first grade?

16. How much homework, if any, should my child have?

17. When should I talk to my child's teacher? When should I talk to the principal?

18. Why should I get involved in my child's classroom or in a parent group like the PTA?

19. How will my child be evaluated? What if she needs special help?

20. What should my child know before moving on to second grade?

Plus ...

A (baker's) dozen things to ask your child's first grade teacher

5 things to look for in the first grade classroom

1 How is first grade different from kindergarten? What are the goals of the first grade classroom?

The first grade classroom your child enters this fall may look very different from or fairly similar to the kindergarten she recently left, depending on the prevailing philosophy and methods of her teacher and school. But the goals for first grade are more or less consistent in most schools across the country.

This year, for the first time, the school's priority for your child may not be socialization, but learning certain content and skills. Strong emphasis will likely be placed on helping your child become a successful reader. Comfort with numbers, writing, spelling, social studies, and science concepts also become important. Work habits are another goal of most first grades. While children are learning the basics of academic subjects, they are also building study skills they can rely upon through their rest of their schooling.

2   What makes a good first grade?

In general, a good first grade is a place where children are encouraged to grow and learn in an active, positive environment. Good first grade teachers help children make the adjustment from kindergarten. Ideally, your child's teacher will observe children to learn about their social/emotional, intellectual, creative, and physical development. She will match her expectations to their capabilities, gradually increasing both over time. Most importantly, a good teacher will make sure every child feels welcomed, accepted, and respected.

At the same time, the skilled first grade teacher is mindful of what children are expected to learn during the year. Through an appropriate balance of whole-group lessons, small-group activities, and individual work, she will plan activities to improve children's reading and math skills and help children understand the world around them. Play in familiar learning centers such as the library, blocks corner, and dramatic-play area will be woven into the fabric of the classroom curriculum.

3 Are all six-year-olds "ready" for first grade? What do I do if my child is not quite ready?

A better way to ask this question may be "Is the school's first grade ready for my child?" Physical development and social/emotional maturity, as well as familiarity with number and letter symbols, can be as important as chronological age in determining whether your child can be successful in first grade. In the best circumstances, first grade teachers individualize their programs to meet each child at his or her appropriate developmental level.

But not all programs are this flexible. If you feel that your child is very immature compared to others her age, and/or if she has delayed language, physical, or interactional skills, consult with your child's teacher and possibly the principal. Discuss whether the regular first grade can meet your child's needs, and what other options are available. Perhaps there is a mixed kindergarten and first grade class, a transitional class, a class where more individualized attention is available, or simply one with a more flexible teacher.

In some rare cases, repeating kindergarten may be a wise choice. This is a difficult decision that should be made as a team by you, the teacher, the principal, and sometimes other specialists. But keep in mind that very few children should be retained. If you notice that a large number of children in your school are being asked to repeat kindergarten, it may indicate an overly rigid first grade. In any case, remember that repeating kindergarten in no way should imply failure on the part of your child or yourself.

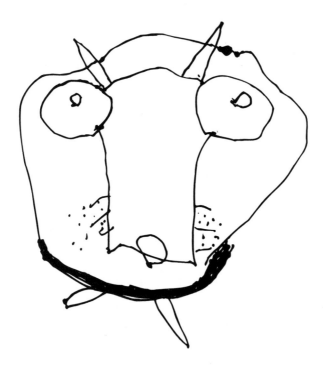

4 What social and emotional challenges will my child meet this year, and what's the best way for me to handle them?

Many of the changes that come with first grade may be challenging to your child. These may include a longer day, more time sitting at a desk, a bigger school, more teachers, and more children of different ages to contend with. Your child may feel intimidated by the older children around him at lunchtime, or worried that he won't be able to find the bus! In addition, some children experience a kind of performance anxiety, especially about reading. They may be concerned that first grade is "serious business" and may wonder: "Can I measure up?"

You can help your child meet these challenges as you would other potential stresses: by preparing him as much as possible and being supportive.

CONSIDER THESE SUGGESTIONS:

- **Visit the classroom ahead of time, if you can.** Together, find the bathroom and other important places in the school. Reassure your child that the teacher and others will help him find any place he needs to go.

- **If your child will ride a bus, take a "dry run" in the car on a relaxed day.** Talk about how long the ride takes and where the bus stops, so he'll know what to expect.

- **If possible, help your child hook up with an older friend** or sibling who can help him find his way around.

- **Be supportive of your child's academic efforts** at whatever level they may be. Avoid comparing him to other children.

- **Avoid adding to his anxiety** by loading on too many new expectations of your own connected with starting first grade.

- **Encourage your child to talk about school.** Try asking specific questions such as: "What were the best and worst things that happened today?"

- **Watch for unspoken signs that your child is having difficulty adjusting.** These may include mood changes, a decline in the quality of work, or attempts to avoid school. If you discover a problem that is school-related, discuss it with your child's teacher.

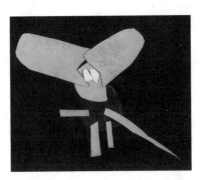

5 What does "developmentally appropriate" mean, and how does it apply to first grade?

"Developmentally appropriate" describes curriculum and teaching methods that are based on how children learn. At the core of developmentally appropriate practice (DAP) is the recognition that children's rates of learning and learning styles vary greatly. Instead of requiring that all the children in a class adapt to one uniform program, teachers who use this approach adapt their program to fit the ages and individual needs of each of the children in their class.

Developmentally appropriate practice is grounded in research about how children learn, and is constantly updated as that knowledge expands. This approach has been used widely in preschools and some kindergartens for many years, and is now being adopted by many primary schools and teachers. The advice in this booklet recognizes the variety of methods your child's first grade teacher might use, while also reinforcing the importance of DAP. You can speak to your child's teacher to find out the extent to which she uses the approach described.

Following are some of the important principles of developmentally appropriate practice as they apply to first grade:

■ **THE "WHOLE CHILD":** Researchers have identified at least five different ways in which children develop: socially, emotionally, physically, creatively, and cognitively or intellectually. All of these domains, not just the cognitive, are included when planning curriculum.

■ **INDIVIDUALIZED LEARNING:** There is a recognition that children learn best at their own pace and that different aspects of children's learning progress at different rates.

■ **INTEGRATED, MEANINGFUL CURRICULUM:** Instead of teaching science, reading, math, or social studies in isolation, children are taught these subjects in the context of a general theme or through projects of interest to them. For example, if your child studies seeds, she will grow seeds, read books about seeds, count and add with seeds, and perhaps create a pretend market to sell seeds. The curriculum content and the materials to teach it relate to your child's and her classmates' actual experiences.

■ **ACTIVE PARTICIPATION:** The curriculum includes large- and small-group activities that empower your child to think, plan, talk, move, and really get involved. It recognizes that children under eight still learn best through hands-on activities.

■ **POSITIVE DISCIPLINE:** Teachers use guidance techniques with the goal not to reward or punish, but to help your child develop self-control.

6 What is the role of cultural diversity in the classroom?

Responding to cultural diversity is another example of developmental appropriateness. Just as your child's classroom should respond to each child's developmental level, it should also be sensitive to each child's cultural background. This can mean race, religion, nationality, or family traditions. True acceptance of cultural diversity is an attitude you can see in the way teachers interact with children and with you, and the way children are expected to interact with one another.

When acceptance is successfully woven into the fabric of a classroom, all children feel respected. Your child's self-esteem and respect for others are enhanced because all traditions are considered valid and valuable.

Culture influences subtle things about how children act. For example, your child might show that he is paying attention to the teacher by looking directly at her, while another child in the same situation shows respect by looking down. In a classroom that embraces diversity, the teacher works to learn about different styles so she can understand children's actions and respond appropriately.

Diversity should also be part of the curriculum. Your first grader may be fascinated by the many ways people live, and for the first time really be able to study them. Through specific activities — and also just by working together — children learn to look for the things people have in common, as well as appreciate differences.

If you feel your child's teacher needs to learn more about your culture, discuss it with her. You can be a great resource!

7   What will my child do all day?

Typically, the first grade day is divided into time segments for different types of activities. Your child should have periods of unstructured outdoor and indoor play, short large-group meetings or lessons, time in learning centers or working on individual projects, and periods to take part in classroom maintenance such as watering plants or updating charts and calendars. Of course there is also time for lunch, and in some first grades, a short rest period. In many schools, the day is divided by walks through the school to special music, art, or gym classes and special events such as assemblies.

In a program with an integrated curriculum, your child may be learning content or study skills during any of these times. For example, outdoor play may include games that develop eye-hand coordination or reinforce the importance of following instructions. Learning-center time may provide an opportunity to use math manipulatives or act out a story. And an art activity may offer her a chance to draw a bird she saw on a class nature walk.

M   maya

8 What is the role of play?

Play is still an important source of learning and enjoyment for your first grader. It provides opportunities for him to interact with others, practice communication and other skills, and develop his sense of competence.

The first grade schedule should include times for play every day. Though play is unstructured, skillful teachers encourage it in all areas of the curriculum. For example, by playing with colored rods your child can discover new number concepts. A dramatic-play area can become a veterinarian's office as part of studying about animals. Building with blocks, children may re-create their school and its surroundings as part of an in-depth investigation about their community. Outdoors, a playground or park serves as a natural science laboratory, and sometimes as a place for games such as "rhyming tag," that reinforce skills.

Through all these play experiences, your child can experiment freely with knowledge and let his imagination go. His teacher, observing children at play, can notice which concepts they understand and which new topics they may be interested in pursuing. The teacher can also gain valuable information about children's social/ emotional development, better enabling her to teach the "whole child."

9 How much choice of activity should my child have in first grade, and how much "seat work" is appropriate?

Children's choices are still of great importance in first grade, and your child should have some degree of choice every day. Many first grades have a period when children can choose activities. The teacher might also let children decide on topics to study. For example, if the class wants to learn about mammals, children might select from a choice of bears, whales, or monkeys. Choices like these should be offered to your child individually, as well as to the class as a group.

"Seat work" usually refers to worksheets and other pencil-and-paper tasks. In good first grade classrooms, however, your child should be using a variety of materials such as math manipulatives and art supplies, even at her desk. How much sitting your child can handle is based somewhat on her motor development and comfort. Most first graders can sit and concentrate better than they could in kindergarten, but still not for extended periods. Your child should be expected to do seat work for no more than about half an hour at a time, and for a total of less than two hours a day. Conversely, many educators who use developmentally appropriate practices don't believe in worksheets for first graders and argue that little seat work should be required. Also, many young children are more comfortable and successful taking traditional seat work to other areas of the room.

10 How will my child learn to read this year?

Children learn the essence of reading through many direct experiences with language and print. When you think about reading, you know that it is more than memorizing the alphabet or recognizing words. Reading is about communication: the process by which your child makes meaning from others' writing. Therefore, exploring oral language through lots of conversation and experimenting with expressive writing are as key to early reading as exploring letter sounds. In good first grades, children learn to read as part of a language and literacy program that is integrated throughout the curriculum. For example, your child may use nonfiction books about birds as part of a science activity, look at picture books about firefighters as part of a social studies theme on community workers, or brainstorm lists of words about the rain forest. Specific reading subskills such as word recognition and phonics may be practiced with the teacher in small groups. Some teachers also meet one-to-one with children to help them learn reading skills using their own writing as the text.

Good books are central to the language and literacy approach. Children are read to daily by teachers and other adults from books carefully selected for their high-quality stories and illustrations. These books are also readily available for children to look at independently in classrooms and school libraries. Listening to and looking at real children's literature, instead of uninteresting "programmed readers," sparks your child's desire to read more. It may not be long before you find your child reading under the covers with a flashlight — not an altogether unwelcome sight!

In recent years the definition of first grade reading has been

broadened to include all the strategies children use to interpret print. When a child "reads" the meaning from the illustrations of a book, he is reading. When he makes a good guess at what a word might mean in the context of a sign, he is reading. Now, instead of correcting mistakes in children's word-for-word reading, teachers (and parents) accept and even celebrate all the steps on the path to literacy.

What if my child doesn't learn to read this year?

It's not the end of the world! And it's certainly not the end of your child's chances for school success. Though many children do begin to read independently during first grade, six- to eight-year-olds naturally vary widely in their development of reading abilities. It's not uncommon for children to begin reading independently in second grade or even later.

If your child is progressing slowly, chances are that by careful observation of specific reading skills, her teacher can pinpoint any areas of difficulty. The teacher can then, if necessary, individualize a program to meet her specific needs.

Remember, too, that the approach to teaching reading in many schools may be different from what you are accustomed to. If you are concerned because you don't see your child reading books on her own, talk with her teacher. If the school is using a developmentally appropriate language and literacy program, it could be that your child is doing fine, developing reading skills at her own pace and in her own way. Often, reading suddenly "clicks" for children, and those who may have learned more slowly in the beginning can read well above grade level or with better comprehension later on.

12 | What is the role of writing in first grade, and what is invented spelling all about?

When you were in first grade, "writing" probably meant "penmanship." But like reading, writing is about communication. It is the art of expressing an idea, feeling, or information on paper.

Writing is an essential part of a good language and literacy program largely because it is so strongly linked to early reading.

In fact, many educators believe that children actually learn to read *through* writing. When they write messages, lists, signs, or stories in the context of other activities, children encounter many basic elements of reading, including spelling, phonics, word usage, and style. Children are better able to decipher and understand others' messages after the experience of writing themselves.

When your child begins to write, it's important that his teachers — and you — accept his work for what it is. If, instead, adults focus on his mistakes in spelling, grammar, or penmanship, he will learn that writing is a physical task or a drill rather than a joyful way of expressing his thoughts. This is part of the idea behind invented spelling. Allowing children to write words in their own ways at the beginning, enables them to focus on their messages, feel confident in their use of print, and actually work harder on their *understanding* of spelling. Later in the first grade year, children generally make the transition from invented spelling to conventional spelling. After this period of experimentation, they become interested in how words are "really spelled" and use the skills they've learned to sound out words or look up spellings in picture dictionaries.

Interestingly, children who have used invented spelling often become better spellers! That's because invented spelling teaches children to think about and problem-solve how to spell a word, instead of relying just on correction and memorization.

13 What math skills might my child learn in first grade?

Some of the math skills your child may be exposed to are:

- addition of numbers 1 through 10

- equality and greater than/less than

- subtraction of numbers 1 through 10

- place value for numbers 1 through 100

- money values

- geometry (evaluating shapes and sizes)

- understanding fractions

- telling time

- reading calendars

- solving word problems

The math program is designed to help children become comfortable using these skills by exploring, discovering, and solving problems of interest to them. For example, they might use addition in the context of a science investigation, or practice reading calendars to find out how many days until an upcoming field trip. Board games and toys such as small blocks or cubes provide endless math possibilities.

Math drills with workbooks or ditto sheets should be used minimally. Learning math facts in isolation can actually keep children from understanding how to apply them. Learning math in context, however, helps your child see how it fits into her life and world.

14 How will my child explore science in first grade?

All children have natural curiosity about the world around them. Your first grader will explore science through special projects, field trips, and items of interest brought into the classroom. He will learn to think like a scientist: asking questions; forming hypotheses; testing possible solutions; and recording his methods, observations, and results. All this can happen through simple classroom activities that increase his understanding of the natural and technological world.

As his use of books and the library expands, he can also begin to "research" topics of special interest to him, such as animals, seashells, or rainbows. You can reinforce his learning with trips to your local public library, science museum, or nature center.

Keeping pets and tending plants are popular science activities that might be part of your child's first grade experience. These projects are part of the classroom routine and help teach responsibility and compassion, as well as science.

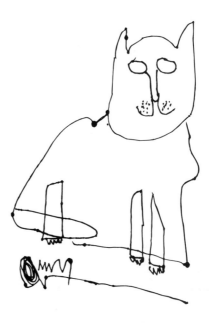

15 What is the role of art and music in first grade?

Genevieve

In a developmentally appropriate first grade, art and music are part of the regular classroom curriculum and the spirit of the classroom, whether or not your child's primary school offers "special" art and music classes. A story may inspire an art project, for example, or provide the song the group chooses to sing that day. Through ongoing art and music activities, your child will appreciate artistic expression and develop her own powerful abilities to create. In addition, both art and music can introduce and reinforce all kinds of learning! For example, math is about shapes and patterns, which your child probably explores quite naturally in her artwork. And songs play with language, tell stories, and have rhythm and rhyme, which all foster literacy skills. Finally, artistic expression helps your child become a more creative thinker and is just plain fun!

16 How much homework, if any, should my child have?

Many developmentally appropriate programs do not give any homework, believing that six- and seven-year-olds need to play and spend special time with their families after a full day of school. Some teachers, though, believe that homework is valuable. If your child does get homework, work with him to make it fun. In general, homework for this age should:

- **BE BRIEF.** Your child should have homework three times a week at the most, and it should require no more than 20 minutes to complete.

- **BE RELATED TO CLASSWORK.** The purpose of homework should be to reinforce what children learned that day, or to lay the foundation for what they'll be covering soon.

- **BE NOT TOO HARD.** Homework in first grade should never be so challenging that it makes children feel anxious, want to avoid it, or feel that they have failed.

- **BE ACKNOWLEDGED.** Your child's teacher should respond to homework promptly. This respects children's efforts and validates the importance of the work they do at home.

17 When should I talk to my child's teacher? When should I talk to the principal?

First ask this question of your child's school when you enroll. Communicating regularly with the teacher helps keep you informed about your child's schooling. Get to know your child's teacher. Express your hopes and expectations for your child's education, and your interest in staying informed about her daily school experiences.

Most schools offer conferences twice a year to discuss children's progress, but you should call at other times if you have questions or concerns. You should also speak to the teacher if your child seems anxious about school or tells you about problems with work, other children, or the teacher herself.

When you speak to the teacher, try to keep your discussion positive and productive. Consider yourselves partners working together for the benefit of your child.

If you speak to your child's teacher about a problem and she is not receptive, or if after a sufficient amount of time the situation does not improve, suggest that together you make an appointment to speak to the teacher's supervisor, usually the principal.

18 Why should I get involved in my child's classroom or in a parent group like the PTA?

Working with the PTA gives you a voice in your child's school experience. It is a vehicle for working with teachers and administrators to help provide your child — and all children in your community — with the best possible education. Increasingly, both parents and professionals are recognizing that parents really are their children's most important teachers. So more than ever, your participation should be sought and valued.

Being involved in the school and in your child's classroom lets him know how important his education is to you. There are many ways for you to help out that both your child and his teacher will welcome. Here are a few suggestions. Ask your teacher for more!

- **Chaperoning field trips**

- **Reading books to children**

- **Assisting with "publishing" (writing, copying, or binding) books children write**

- **Sharing something about your culture**

- **Conducting special activities (or routine ones)**

- **Making learning materials**

19 How will my child be evaluated? What if she needs special help?

Some schools make use of standardized tests, which are uniform measurement tools administered to children according to specified procedures. Child development professionals, however, argue strongly that in most cases, standardized tests are ineffective for evaluating first graders.

As an alternative, your school may use a method known as portfolio assessment, in which teachers collect written or recorded examples of your child's work, along with detailed notes they've made while observing your child's activities. Portfolio assessment yields a broader, deeper look at your child's overall progress than can be gained from a pencil-and-paper test. Portfolios also offer you a wonderful window into your child's work at conference time.

When reviewing portfolios, teachers may notice specific areas of development in which children need additional help. At that point, more standardized screening or diagnostic measures may become appropriate. If your teacher recommends this for your child, be sure she explains her reasons and the testing process in detail. Discuss what the outcomes might be. If the tests indicate that your child has any special needs, the school must provide the remedial help she requires to be a successful learner.

20 What should my child know before moving on to second grade?

There are no universal "must-knows" for first graders. Most schools have identified a core of information for first grade teachers to cover, usually including such things as specific "sight words" for children to recognize, basic addition and subtractions facts, and science and social studies content areas. You can learn more about your school's first grade curriculum goals from your child's teacher or principal.

More important than what information children learn is how they learn to approach it. Following are some skills that your child should be developing this year:

■ **THINKING SKILLS** — including the ability to use information to solve a problem, to look at objects and situations in different ways, to analyze information and make judgments about it, and to form and test hypotheses.

■ **STUDY SKILLS** — including the ability to concentrate, to listen, to follow directions, and to find answers to questions independently.

■ **MOTIVATION** — including an excitement about learning, a desire to meet new learning challenges, and the confidence to be creative and take risks.

If your child is able to apply these skills in his current classroom, you can feel comfortable that he has what he needs to meet the challenges of second grade — and beyond!

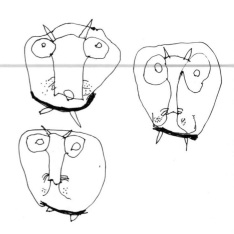

A (baker's) dozen
things to ask
your child's first grade teacher

1. What are your goals for the children in the class this year? How do you think you can best meet them?

2. Can you suggest ways for me to help my child feel comfortable interacting with older children on the bus and in the lunchroom? Do you teach social problem-solving skills in the classroom?

3. What is your approach to discipline? How do you handle children who are disruptive?

4. What is your approach to diversity and multiculturalism in the classroom? How will my child's culture be represented and respected?

5. How many children are there in the class? How many teachers or aides?

6. How many "specials" (gym, art, music, library) will my child attend each week? Will these classes be held in the regular classroom or in other parts of the building?

7. How much time will children spend learning in large groups and how much time working in small groups or independently?

8. How much time each day will my child be working on pencil-and-paper tasks or worksheets? How much free choice will she have?

9. What approaches do you use to teach reading? How can I help my child with reading at home?

10. Will you be giving my child work to do at home? How can I help my child with homework?

11. What's the best way for us to keep in touch? Can you be reached by phone?

12. How can I help in the classroom in the time I have available? Is there something I can do outside of school to help the class?

13. Is there a written policy regarding school closings, emergencies, illnesses in school, vacations, and transportation? How can I get a copy?